3

## SIZE INFORMATION

**Size:** 3-6 months
**Finished Measurements:**
  Diaper Cover - 14$^1$/$_2$" (37 cm)
    long with an adjustable waist
  Hat - 15" (38 cm) circumference

## GAUGE INFORMATION

6 dc and 4 rows/rnds = 2" (5 cm)
**Gauge Swatch:** 3$^1$/$_4$" wide x 3" high
  (8.25 cm x 7.5 cm)
With White, ch 11.
**Row 1:** Dc in third ch from hook and
in each ch across: 9 dc.
**Rows 2-6:** Ch 2 (does **not** count as
a dc), turn; dc in first dc and in each
dc across.
Finish off.

## ───── STITCH GUIDE ─────
### DOUBLE CROCHET 2 TOGETHER
  *(abbreviated dc2tog)* (uses 2 sts)
★ YO, insert hook in **next** st, YO and
pull up a loop, YO and draw through
2 loops on hook; repeat from ★
once **more**, YO and draw through all
3 loops on hook (**counts as one dc**).

## INSTRUCTIONS
## Diaper Cover

With White and beginning at waist,
ch 67.

**Row 1** (Right side)**:** Dc in third ch
from hook and in each ch across:
65 dc.

*Note:* Loop a short piece of yarn
around any stitch to mark Row 1 as
**right** side.

**Row 2:** Ch 2 (does **not** count as a
dc, now and throughout), turn; dc in
first dc and in each dc across.

**Row 3** (Buttonhole row)**:** Ch 2, turn;
dc in first dc, ch 1, (skip next dc, dc
in next 3 dc, ch 1) twice, skip next
dc, dc in next 45 dc, ch 1, (skip next
dc, dc in next 3 dc, ch 1) twice, skip
next dc, dc in last dc: 59 dc and
6 buttonholes (ch-1 sps).

**Row 4:** Ch 2, turn; dc in first dc
and in each dc and in each ch-1 sp
across: 65 dc.

# Hats & Diaper Covers

LEISURE ARTS, INC. • Little Rock, Arkansas

# BUNNY SET

◼️◻️◻️◻️▷ **BEGINNER +**

---

## SHOPPING LIST

**Yarn** (Medium Weight) 🧶4
[6 ounces, 315 yards
(170 grams, 288 meters) per skein]:
- ☐ White - 1 skein
- ☐ Pink - 50 yards (45.5 meters)
- ☐ Black - small amount for face

## Crochet Hook
- ☐ Size I (5.5 mm)
  **or** size needed for gauge

## Additional Supplies
- ☐ 1-1¼" (25-32 mm) Button
- ☐ Snaps - 2 **or** 6 (to make the diaper cover adjustable)
- ☐ Yarn needle
- ☐ Sewing needle and matching thread

**Row 5:** Ch 2, turn; dc in first dc and in each dc across.

**Row 6:** Turn; slip st loosely in first 18 dc, ch 2, dc in next 29 dc, leave remaining 18 dc unworked: 29 dc.

**Rows 7-13** (Decrease rows)**:** Ch 2, turn; beginning in first dc, dc2tog, dc in next dc and in each dc across to last 2 dc, dc2tog: 15 dc.

**Rows 14 and 15:** Ch 2, turn; dc in first dc and in each dc across.

**Rows 16-20** (Increase rows)**:** Ch 2, turn; 2 dc in first dc, dc in next dc and in each dc across to last dc, 2 dc in last dc: 25 dc.

**Rows 21-28:** Ch 2, turn; dc in first dc and in each dc across; do **not** finish off.

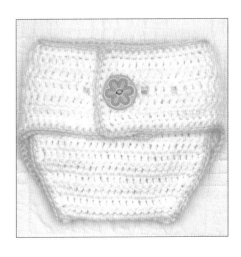

## EDGING

**Rnd 1:** Ch 1, do **not** turn; sc evenly around entire piece working *(Fig. 1, page 43)* 3 sc in each corner; join with slip st to first sc, finish off.

**Rnd 2:** With **right** side facing, join Pink with sc in same st as joining *(Figs. 2a & b, page 44)*; sc in next sc and in each sc around working 3 sc in each corner sc; join with slip st to first sc, finish off.

## BUTTONS & SNAPS PLACEMENT

With **right** side facing, sew button to center of Row 26 (front). The front can be buttoned in any of the 3 buttonholes on each side for an adjustable fit.

Snaps are added to keep the corners of the last row in place. Sew a half snap on the **right** side of each corner of Row 28.

Button the diaper cover in the desired position, then sew the second half of each snap on the **wrong** side of Row 1 to correspond with the first half of the snap. For the diaper cover to be adjustable, the second half of 2 additional snaps may be sewn on each side of Row 1 to match the first half of the snap when the cover is buttoned in the remaining 2 buttonhole choices.

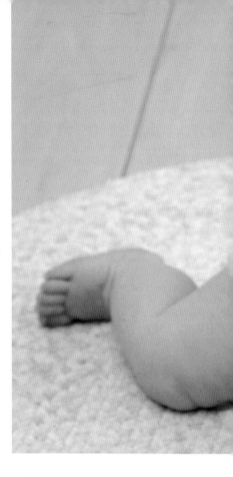

## Hat

With White, ch 4; join with slip st to form a ring.

**Rnd 1** (Right side)**:** Ch 2 (does **not** count as a dc, now and throughout), 12 dc in ring; join with slip st to first dc: 12 dc.

*Note:* Loop a short piece of yarn around any stitch to mark Rnd 1 as **right** side.

**Rnd 2:** Ch 2, do **not** turn; 2 dc in same st as joining and in each dc around; join with slip st to first dc: 24 dc.

**Rnd 3:** Ch 2, dc in same st as joining, 2 dc in next dc, (dc in next dc, 2 dc in next dc) around; join with slip st to first dc: 36 dc.

**Rnd 4:** Ch 2, dc in same st as joining and in next 2 dc, 2 dc in next dc, (dc in next 3 dc, 2 dc in next dc) around; join with slip st to first dc: 45 dc.

**Rnd 5:** Ch 2, dc in same st as joining and in each dc around; join with slip st to first dc.

Repeat Rnd 5, 7 times **or** until Hat measures desired length.

**Edging:** Ch 1, sc in same st as joining and in each dc around; join with slip st to first sc, finish off.

## EAR (Make 2)
Each Ear is made in two pieces.

### OUTER EAR
With White, ch 8.

**Row 1** (Right side)**:** Dc in third ch from hook and in each ch across: 6 dc.

*Note:* Mark Row 1 as **right** side.

**Rows 2-11:** Ch 2, turn; dc in first dc and in each dc across.

**Row 12:** Ch 2, turn; beginning in first dc, dc2tog, dc in next 2 dc, dc2tog: 4 dc.

**Row 13:** Ch 2, turn; beginning in first dc, dc2tog twice; finish off: 2 dc.

### INNER EAR
With Pink, work same as Outer Ear.

With **wrong** sides of both pieces together and using White, sew around entire edge to join.

Using photo as a guide for placement, sew Ears between Rnds 2 and 3 on each side of Hat.

Using photo as a guide, embroider face using Pink satin stitch for nose, Black satin stitch for eyes, and Black straight stitches for whiskers *(see Embroidery Stitches, page 46)*.

# CHICK SET

 **BEGINNER +**

---

## SHOPPING LIST

**Yarn** (Medium Weight) 🧶 **4**
**[7 ounces, 364 yards
(198 grams, 333 meters) per skein]:**
☐ Yellow - 1 skein
☐ Orange - 10 yards (9 meters)

### Crochet Hook
☐ Size I (5.5 mm)
**or** size needed for gauge

### Additional Supplies
☐ 1-1$^1$/$_4$" (25-32 mm) Button
☐ $^3$/$_8$" (10 mm) Round buttons -
2 **or** black yarn to
embroider eyes
☐ Snaps - 2 **or** 6 (to make the
diaper cover adjustable)
☐ Yarn needle
☐ Sewing needle and matching
thread

## SIZE INFORMATION

**Size:** 3-6 months
**Finished Measurements:**
   Diaper Cover - 14¼" (36 cm)
     long with an adjustable waist
   Hat - 18" (45.5 cm) circumference

## GAUGE INFORMATION

6 dc and 4 rows/rnds = 2" (5 cm)
**Gauge Swatch:** 3¼" wide x 3" high
   (8.25 cm x 7.5 cm)
With Yellow, ch 11.
**Row 1:** Dc in third ch from hook and in each ch across: 9 dc.
**Rows 2-6:** Ch 2 (does **not** count as a dc), turn; dc in first dc and in each dc across.
Finish off.

## ——— STITCH GUIDE ———

**DOUBLE CROCHET 2 TOGETHER**
   *(abbreviated dc2tog)* (uses 2 sts)
★ YO, insert hook in **next** st, YO and pull up a loop, YO and draw through 2 loops on hook; repeat from ★ once **more**, YO and draw through all 3 loops on hook (**counts as one dc**).

## INSTRUCTIONS
# Diaper Cover

With Yellow and beginning at waist, ch 67.

**Row 1:** Dc in third ch from hook and in each ch across: 65 dc.

**Row 2** (Right side)**:** Ch 2 (does **not** count as a dc, now and throughout), turn; dc in first dc and in each dc across.

*Note:* Loop a short piece of yarn around any stitch to mark Row 2 as **right** side.

**Row 3** (Buttonhole row)**:** Ch 2, turn; dc in first dc, ch 1, (skip next dc, dc in next 3 dc, ch 1) twice, skip next dc, dc in next 45 dc, ch 1, (skip next dc, dc in next 3 dc, ch 1) twice, skip next dc, dc in last dc: 59 dc and 6 buttonholes (ch-1 sps).

**Row 4:** Ch 2, turn; dc in first dc and in each dc and in each ch-1 sp across: 65 dc.

**Row 5:** Ch 2, turn; dc in first dc and in each dc across.

**Row 6:** Turn; slip st loosely in first 18 dc, ch 2, dc in next 29 dc, leave remaining 18 dc unworked: 29 dc.

**Rows 7-13** (Decrease rows)**:** Ch 2, turn; beginning in first dc, dc2tog, dc in next dc and in each dc across to last 2 dc, dc2tog: 15 dc.

**Rows 14 and 15:** Ch 2, turn; dc in first dc and in each dc across.

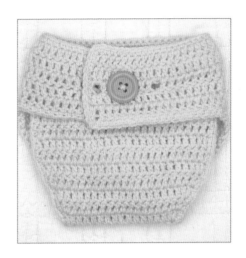

**Rows 16-20** (Increase rows)**:** Ch 2, turn; 2 dc in first dc, dc in next dc and in each dc across to last dc, 2 dc in last dc: 25 dc.

**Rows 21-28:** Ch 2, turn; dc in first dc and in each dc across; do **not** finish off.

**Edging:** Ch 1, do **not** turn; sc evenly around entire piece *(Fig. 1, page 43)* working 3 sc in each corner; join with slip st to first sc, finish off.

**BUTTONS & SNAPS PLACEMENT**
With **right** side facing, sew button to center of Row 26 (front). The front can be buttoned in any of the 3 buttonholes on each side for an adjustable fit.

Snaps are added to keep the corners of the last row in place. Sew a half snap on the **right** side of each corner of Row 28.
Button the diaper cover in the desired position, then sew the second half of each snap on the **wrong** side of Row 1 to correspond with the first half of the snap. For the diaper cover to be adjustable, the second half of 2 additional snaps may be sewn on each side of Row 1 to match the first half of the snap when the cover is buttoned in the remaining 2 buttonhole choices.

## Hat

With Yellow, ch 4; join with slip st to form a ring.

**Rnd 1** (Right side): Ch 2 (does **not** count as a dc, now and throughout), 12 dc in ring; join with slip st to first dc: 12 dc.

*Note:* Loop a short piece of yarn around any stitch to mark Rnd 1 as **right** side.

**Rnd 2:** Ch 2, do **not** turn; 2 dc in same st as joining and in each dc around; join with slip st to first dc: 24 dc.

**Rnd 3:** Ch 2, dc in same st as joining, 2 dc in next dc, (dc in next dc, 2 dc in next dc) around; join with slip st to first dc: 36 dc.

**Rnd 4:** Ch 2, dc in same st as joining and in next 2 dc, 2 dc in next dc, (dc in next 3 dc, 2 dc in next dc) around; join with slip st to first dc: 45 dc.

**Rnd 5:** Ch 2, dc in same st as joining and in each dc around; join with slip st to first dc.

**Rnd 6:** Ch 2, dc in same st as joining and in next 3 dc, 2 dc in next dc, (dc in next 4 dc, 2 dc in next dc) around; join with slip st to first dc: 54 dc.

**Rnd 7:** Ch 2, dc in same st as joining and in each dc around; join with slip st to first dc.

Repeat Rnd 7, 6 times **or** until Hat measures desired length; do **not** finish off.

## FIRST EAR FLAP

**Row 1:** Ch 2, do **not** turn; dc in same st as joining and in next 9 dc, leave remaining 44 dc unworked: 10 dc.

**Row 2:** Ch 2, turn; skip first dc, dc in next 7 dc, dc2tog: 8 dc.

**Row 3:** Ch 2, turn; skip first dc, dc in next 5 dc, dc2tog: 6 dc.

**Row 4:** Ch 2, turn; skip first dc, dc in next 3 dc, dc2tog: 4 dc.

**Row 5:** Ch 2, turn; skip first dc, dc in next dc, dc2tog: 2 dc.

**Tie:** Turn; slip st in first dc, ch 40; finish off.

## SECOND EAR FLAP

**Row 1:** With **right** side of Hat facing, skip next 9 dc from First Ear flap and loop a short piece of yarn around next dc to mark center front, skip next 9 dc and join Yellow with dc in next dc *(Fig. 3, page 44)*; dc in next 9 dc, leave remaining 15 dc unworked: 10 dc.

**Row 2:** Ch 2, turn; skip first dc, dc in next 7 dc, dc2tog: 8 dc.

**Row 3:** Ch 2, turn; skip first dc, dc in next 5 dc, dc2tog: 6 dc.

**Row 4:** Ch 2, turn; skip first dc, dc in next 3 dc, dc2tog: 4 dc.

**Row 5:** Ch 2, turn; skip first dc, dc in next dc, dc2tog: 2 dc.

**Tie:** Turn; slip st in first dc, ch 40; finish off.

Using Orange, make 2 tassels *(Figs. 4a & b, page 45)* and attach one to end of each Tie.

## BEAK

With Orange, ch 4; join with slip st to form a ring.

**Rnd 1** (Right side): Ch 1, 8 sc in ring; join with slip st to first sc.

*Note:* Mark Rnd 1 as **right** side.

**Rnd 2:** Ch 1, do **not** turn; sc in same st as joining, 2 sc in next sc, (sc in next sc, 2 sc in next sc) 3 times; join with slip st to first sc: 12 sc.

**Rnd 3:** Ch 1, sc in same st as joining and in each sc around; join with slip st to first sc.

**Rnd 4:** Ch 1, sc in same st as joining and in next 2 sc, 2 sc in next sc, (sc in next 3 sc, 2 sc in next sc) twice; join with slip st to first sc: 15 sc.

**Rnd 5:** Ch 1, sc in same st as joining and in each sc around; join with slip st to first sc, finish off leaving a long end for sewing.

Using photo as a guide for placement and long end, sew Beak to front of Hat between Rnds 8 and 12, lining up center of Beak with marked dc on last rnd of Hat.

Sew round buttons to front of Hat **or** embroider eyes using Black satin stitch *(Figs. 5a & b, page 46)*.

*Note:* Please take caution when using buttons as they may present a choking hazard for infants.

Cut 11 strands of Yellow, each 2" (5 cm) long.
Using a 6" (15 cm) length of Yellow, tie the strands together at the center and attach to top of Hat.

# PUPPY SET

 **BEGINNER +**

## SHOPPING LIST

### Yarn (Medium Weight)
[5 ounces, 260 yards
(141 grams, 238 meters) per skein]:
☐ Ecru (fleck) - 1 skein
☐ Brown - 65 yards (59.5 meters)
☐ Black - small amount for face

### Crochet Hook
☐ Size I (5.5 mm)
**or** size needed for gauge

### Additional Supplies
☐ 1-1¹/₄" (25-32 mm) Button
☐ Snaps - 2 **or** 6 (to make the
diaper cover adjustable)
☐ Yarn needle
☐ Sewing needle and matching
thread

# SIZE INFORMATION

**Size:** 3-6 months
**Finished Measurements:**
Diaper Cover - 14$^1$/$_2$" (37 cm)
long with an adjustable waist
Hat - 15" (38 cm) circumference

# GAUGE INFORMATION

6 dc and 4 rows/rnds = 2" (5 cm)
**Gauge Swatch:** 3$^1$/$_4$" wide x 3" high
(8.25 cm x 7.5 cm)
With Ecru, ch 11.
**Row 1:** Dc in third ch from hook and
in each ch across: 9 dc.
**Rows 2-6:** Ch 2 (does **not** count as
a dc), turn; dc in first dc and in each
dc across.
Finish off.

## ——— STITCH GUIDE ———

**DOUBLE CROCHET 2 TOGETHER**
*(abbreviated dc2tog)* (uses 2 sts)
★ YO, insert hook in **next** st, YO and
pull up a loop, YO and draw through
2 loops on hook; repeat from ★
once **more**, YO and draw through all
3 loops on hook (**counts as one dc**).

# INSTRUCTIONS
# Diaper Cover

With Ecru and beginning at waist,
ch 67.

**Row 1** (Right side)**:** Dc in third ch
from hook and in each ch across:
65 dc.

*Note:* Loop a short piece of yarn
around any stitch to mark Row 1 as
**right** side.

**Row 2:** Ch 2 (does **not** count as a
dc, now and throughout), turn; dc in
first dc and in each dc across.

**Row 3** (Buttonhole row)**:** Ch 2, turn;
dc in first dc, ch 1, (skip next dc, dc
in next 3 dc, ch 1) twice, skip next
dc, dc in next 45 dc, ch 1, (skip next
dc, dc in next 3 dc, ch 1) twice, skip
next dc, dc in last dc: 59 dc and
6 buttonholes (ch-1 sps).

**Row 4:** Ch 2, turn; dc in first dc
and in each dc and in each ch-1 sp
across: 65 dc.

**Row 5:** Ch 2, turn; dc in first dc and in each dc across.

**Row 6:** Turn; slip st loosely in first 18 dc, ch 2, dc in next 29 dc, leave remaining 18 dc unworked: 29 dc.

**Rows 7-13** (Decrease rows)**:** Ch 2, turn; beginning in first dc, dc2tog, dc in next dc and in each dc across to last 2 dc, dc2tog: 15 dc.

**Rows 14 and 15:** Ch 2, turn; dc in first dc and in each dc across.

**Rows 16-20** (Increase rows)**:** Ch 2, turn; 2 dc in first dc, dc in next dc and in each dc across to last dc, 2 dc in last dc: 25 dc.

**Rows 21-28:** Ch 2, turn; dc in first dc and in each dc across; do **not** finish off.

## EDGING

**Rnd 1:** Ch 1, do **not** turn; sc evenly around entire piece *(Fig. 1, page 43)* working 3 sc in each corner; join with slip st to first sc, finish off.

**Rnd 2:** With **right** side facing, join Brown with sc in same st as joining *(Figs. 2a & b, page 44)*; sc in next sc and in each sc around working 3 sc in each corner sc; join with slip st to first sc, finish off.

## BUTTONS & SNAPS PLACEMENT

With **right** side facing, sew button to center of Row 26 (front). The front can be buttoned in any of the 3 buttonholes on each side for an adjustable fit.

Snaps are added to keep the corners of the last row in place. Sew a half snap on the **right** side of each corner of Row 28.

Button the diaper cover in the desired position, then sew the second half of each snap on the **wrong** side of Row 1 to correspond with the first half of the snap.

For the diaper cover to be adjustable, the second half of 2 additional snaps may be sewn on each side of Row 1 to match the first half of the snap when the cover is buttoned in the remaining 2 buttonhole choices.

## PATCH

With Brown, ch 6.

**Rnd 1** (Right side)**:** 3 Sc in second ch from hook, sc in next 3 chs, 3 sc in last ch; working in free loops of beginning ch, sc in next 3 chs; join with slip st to first sc: 12 sc.

*Note:* Mark Rnd 1 as **right** side.

**Rnd 2:** Ch 1, do **not** turn; 2 sc in same st as joining and in each of next 2 sc, sc in next 3 sc, 2 sc in each of next 3 sc, sc in last 3 sc; join with slip st to first sc: 18 sc.

**Rnd 3:** Ch 1, sc in same st as joining, 2 sc in next sc, (sc in next sc, 2 sc in next sc) twice, sc in next 4 sc, 2 sc in next sc, (sc in next sc, 2 sc in next sc) twice, sc in last 3 sc; join with slip st to first sc: 24 sc.

**Rnd 4:** Ch 1, sc in same st as joining and in next sc, 2 sc in next sc, (sc in next 2 sc, 2 sc in next sc) twice, sc in next 5 sc, 2 sc in next sc, (sc in next 2 sc, 2 sc in next sc) twice, sc in last 3 sc; join with slip st to first sc: 30 sc.

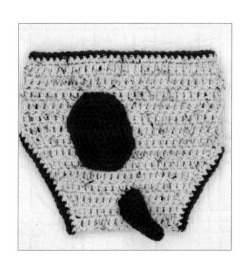

**Rnd 5:** Ch 1, sc in same st as joining and in next 2 sc, 2 sc in next sc, (sc in next 3 sc, 2 sc in next sc) twice, sc in next 6 sc, (2 sc in next sc, sc in next 3 sc) 3 times; join with slip st to first sc, finish off leaving a long end for sewing: 36 sc.

## TAIL

With Brown, ch 4; join with slip st to form a ring.

**Rnd 1** (Right side)**:** Ch 1, 6 sc in ring; do **not** join.

*Note:* Mark Rnd 1 as **right** side.

Place a 2" (5 cm) scrap piece of yarn before the first stitch of round, moving the marker after each round is complete.

**Rnds 2-4:** Sc in each sc around.

**Rnds 5-10** (Increase rnds)**:** 2 Sc in next sc, sc in next sc and in each sc around: 12 sc.

Slip st in next sc, finish off leaving a long end for sewing.

Using photo as a guide for placement and long end, sew Patch and Tail to back of Diaper Cover.

# Hat

With Ecru, ch 4; join with slip st to form a ring.

**Rnd 1** (Right side)**:** Ch 2 (does **not** count as a dc, now and throughout), 12 dc in ring; join with slip st to first dc: 12 dc.

*Note:* Loop a short piece of yarn around any stitch to mark Rnd 1 as **right** side.

**Rnd 2:** Ch 2, do **not** turn; 2 dc in same st as joining and in each dc around; join with slip st to first dc: 24 dc.

**Rnd 3:** Ch 2, dc in same st as joining, 2 dc in next dc, (dc in next dc, 2 dc in next dc) around; join with slip st to first dc: 36 dc.

**Rnd 4:** Ch 2, dc in same st as joining and in next 2 dc, 2 dc in next dc, (dc in next 3 dc, 2 dc in next dc) around; join with slip st to first dc: 45 dc.

**Rnd 5:** Ch 2, dc in same st as joining and in each dc around; join with slip st to first dc.

Repeat Rnd 5, 6 times **or** until Hat measures desired length.

**Edging:** Ch 1, sc in same st as joining and in each dc around; join with slip st to first sc, finish off.

## EYE PATCH

With Brown, ch 4; join with slip st to form a ring.

**Rnd 1** (Right side)**:** Ch 1, 7 sc in ring; join with slip st to first sc.

*Note:* Mark Rnd 1 as **right** side.

**Rnd 2:** Ch 1, do **not** turn; 2 sc in same st as joining and in each sc around; join with slip st to first sc: 14 sc.

**Rnd 3:** Ch 1, sc in same st as joining and in next sc, (2 sc in next sc, sc in next 2 sc) around; join with slip st to first sc: 18 sc.

**Rnd 4:** Ch 1, sc in same st as joining and in next sc, (2 sc in next sc, sc in next 3 sc) around; join with slip st to first sc, finish off leaving a long end for sewing: 22 sc.

# EAR (Make 1 Ecru and 1 Brown)
Ch 4; join with slip st to form a ring.

**Rnd 1** (Right side): Ch 2, 8 dc in ring; join with slip st to first dc.

*Note:* Mark Rnd 1 as **right** side.

**Rnd 2:** Ch 2, do **not** turn; dc in same st as joining, 2 dc in next dc, (dc in next dc, 2 dc in next dc) 3 times; join with slip st to first dc: 12 dc.

**Rnd 3:** Ch 2, dc in same st as joining and in next 2 dc, 2 dc in next dc, (dc in next 3 dc, 2 dc in next dc) twice; join with slip st to first dc: 15 dc.

**Rnd 4:** Ch 2, dc in same st as joining and in next 3 dc, 2 dc in next dc, (dc in next 4 dc, 2 dc in next dc) twice; join with slip st to first dc: 18 dc.

**Rnds 5-7:** Ch 2, dc in same st as joining and in each dc around; join with slip st to first dc.

Finish off leaving a long end for sewing.

Using photo as a guide for placement and long end, sew Eye Patch and Ears to Hat, placing Ears between Rnds 2 and 3.

Using photo as a guide, embroider face using Black satin stitch for nose and eyes *(Figs. 5a & b, page 46).*

# LADYBUG SET

 **BEGINNER +**

## SHOPPING LIST

**Yarn** (Medium Weight) 🔵4 MEDIUM
**[7 ounces, 364 yards
(198 grams, 333 meters) per skein]:**
☐ Red - 1 skein
☐ Black - 40 yards (36.5 meters)

### Crochet Hook
☐ Size I (5.5 mm)
   **or** size needed for gauge

### Additional Supplies
☐ 1-1¹/₄" (25-32 mm) Button
☐ Snaps - 2 **or** 6 (to make the
   diaper cover adjustable)
☐ Yarn needle
☐ Sewing needle and matching
   thread

## SIZE INFORMATION

**Size:** 3-6 months
**Finished Measurements:**
   Diaper Cover - 14$\frac{1}{4}$" (36 cm)
      long with an adjustable waist
   Hat - 15" (38 cm) circumference

## GAUGE INFORMATION

6 dc and 4 rows/rnds = 2" (5 cm)
**Gauge Swatch:** 3$\frac{1}{4}$" wide x 3" high
   (8.25 cm x 7.5 cm)
With Red, ch 11.
**Row 1:** Dc in third ch from hook and
in each ch across: 9 dc.
**Rows 2-6:** Ch 2 (does **not** count as
a dc), turn; dc in first dc and in each
dc across.
Finish off.

## ──── STITCH GUIDE ────

**DOUBLE CROCHET 2 TOGETHER**
   *(abbreviated dc2tog) (uses 2 sts)*
★ YO, insert hook in **next** st, YO and
pull up a loop, YO and draw through
2 loops on hook; repeat from ★
once **more**, YO and draw through all
3 loops on hook (**counts as one dc**).

## INSTRUCTIONS
## Diaper Cover

With Red and beginning at waist,
ch 67.

**Row 1:** Dc in third ch from hook and
in each ch across: 65 dc.

**Row 2** (Right side)**:** Ch 2 (does **not**
count as a dc, now and throughout),
turn; dc in first dc and in each dc
across.

*Note:* Loop a short piece of yarn
around any stitch to mark Row 2 as
**right** side.

**Row 3** (Buttonhole row)**:** Ch 2, turn;
dc in first dc, ch 1, (skip next dc, dc
in next 3 dc, ch 1) twice, skip next
dc, dc in next 45 dc, ch 1, (skip next
dc, dc in next 3 dc, ch 1) twice, skip
next dc, dc in last dc: 59 dc and
6 buttonholes (ch-1 sps).

**Row 4:** Ch 2, turn; dc in first dc
and in each dc and in each ch-1 sp
across: 65 dc.

**Row 5:** Ch 2, turn; dc in first dc and
in each dc across.

**Row 6:** Turn; slip st loosely in first
18 dc, ch 2, dc in next 29 dc, leave
remaining 18 dc unworked: 29 dc.

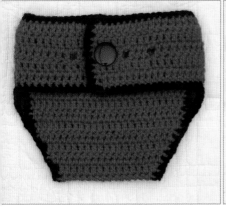

**Rows 7-13** (Decrease rows): Ch 2, turn; beginning in first dc, dc2tog, dc in next dc and in each dc across to last 2 dc, dc2tog: 15 dc.

**Rows 14 and 15:** Ch 2, turn; dc in first dc and in each dc across.

**Rows 16-20** (Increase rows): Ch 2, turn; 2 dc in first dc, dc in next dc and in each dc across to last dc, 2 dc in last dc: 25 dc.

**Rows 21-28:** Ch 2, turn; dc in first dc and in each dc across.

Finish off.

**Edging:** With **right** side facing, join Black with sc in first st *(Figs. 2a & b, page 44)*; sc evenly around entire piece working 3 sc in each corner; join with slip st to first sc, finish off.

**BUTTONS & SNAPS PLACEMENT**
With **right** side facing, sew button to center of Row 26 (front). The front can be buttoned in any of the 3 buttonholes on each side for an adjustable fit.

Snaps are added to keep the corners of the last row in place. Sew a half snap on the **right** side of each corner of Row 28.
Button the diaper cover in the desired position, then sew the second half of each snap on the **wrong** side of Row 1 to correspond with the first half of the snap.
For the diaper cover to be adjustable, the second half of 2 additional snaps may be sewn on each side of Row 1 to match the first half of the snap when the cover is buttoned in the remaining 2 buttonhole choices.

## DOT (Make 4)

With Black, ch 4; join with slip st to form a ring.

**Rnd 1** (Right side): Ch 2, 12 dc in ring; join with slip st to first dc, finish off leaving a long end for sewing.

*Note:* Mark Rnd 1 as **right** side.

Using photo, page 31, as a guide for placement and long end, sew Dots on back of Diaper Cover.

# Hat

With Red, ch 4; join with slip st to form a ring.

**Rnd 1** (Right side): Ch 2 (does **not** count as a dc, now and throughout), 12 dc in ring; join with slip st to first dc: 12 dc.

*Note:* Loop a short piece of yarn around any stitch to mark Rnd 1 as **right** side.

**Rnd 2:** Ch 2, do **not** turn; 2 dc in same st as joining and in each dc around; join with slip st to first dc: 24 dc.

**Rnd 3:** Ch 2, dc in same st as joining, 2 dc in next dc, (dc in next dc, 2 dc in next dc) around; join with slip st to first dc: 36 dc.

**Rnd 4:** Ch 2, dc in same st as joining and in next 2 dc, 2 dc in next dc, (dc in next 3 dc, 2 dc in next dc) around; join with slip st to first dc: 45 dc.

**Rnd 5:** Ch 2, dc in same st as joining and in each dc around; join with slip st to first dc.

Repeat Rnd 5, 6 times **or** until Hat measures desired length; finish off

**Edging:** With **right** side facing, join Black with sc in same st as joining *(Figs. 2a & b, page 44)*; sc in next dc and in each dc around; join with slip st to first sc, finish off.

## DOT (Make 6)

With Black, ch 4; join with slip st to form a ring.

**Rnd 1** (Right side): Ch 2, 12 dc in ring; join with slip st to first dc, finish off leaving a long end for sewing.

*Note:* Mark Rnd 1 as **right** side.

## ANTENNA (Make 2)

With Black, ch 10; slip st in second ch from hook and in each ch across; finish off leaving a long end for sewing.

Using photo as a guide for placement and long end, sew Dots on Hat. Sew each Antenna to top of Hat between Rnds 1 and 2.

# GIRAFFE SET

 **BEGINNER +**

## SHOPPING LIST

**Yarn** (Medium Weight)
[3 ounces, 160 yards
(85 grams, 146 meters) per skein]**:**
- ☐ Gold - 2 skeins
- ☐ Brown - 30 yards (27.5 meters)

### Crochet Hook
- ☐ Size I (5.5 mm)
  **or** size needed for gauge

### Additional Supplies
- ☐ Polyester fiberfill - small amount
- ☐ 1-1¼" (25-32 mm) Button
- ☐ Snaps - 2 **or** 6 (to make the
  diaper cover adjustable)
- ☐ Yarn needle
- ☐ Sewing needle and matching
  thread

# SIZE INFORMATION

**Size:** 3-6 months
**Finished Measurements:**
  Diaper Cover - $14^1/_2$" (37 cm)
    long with an adjustable waist
  Hat - 15" (38 cm) circumference

# GAUGE INFORMATION

6 dc and 4 rows/rnds = 2" (5 cm)
**Gauge Swatch:** $3^1/_4$" wide x 3" high
  (8.25 cm x 7.5 cm)
With Gold, ch 11.
**Row 1:** Dc in third ch from hook and
in each ch across: 9 dc.
**Rows 2-6:** Ch 2 (does **not** count as
a dc), turn; dc in first dc and in each
dc across.
Finish off.

## ──── STITCH GUIDE ────

**DOUBLE CROCHET 2 TOGETHER**
  *(abbreviated dc2tog)* (uses 2 sts)
★ YO, insert hook in **next** st, YO and
pull up a loop, YO and draw through
2 loops on hook; repeat from ★
once **more**, YO and draw through all
3 loops on hook (**counts as one dc**).

# INSTRUCTIONS
# Diaper Cover

With Gold and beginning at waist,
ch 67.

**Row 1** (Right side)**:** Dc in third ch
from hook and in each ch across:
65 dc.

*Note:* Loop a short piece of yarn
around any stitch to mark Row 1 as
**right** side.

**Row 2:** Ch 2 (does **not** count as a
dc, now and throughout), turn; dc in
first dc and in each dc across.

**Row 3** (Buttonhole row)**:** Ch 2, turn;
dc in first dc, ch 1, (skip next dc, dc
in next 3 dc, ch 1) twice, skip next
dc, dc in next 45 dc, ch 1, (skip next
dc, dc in next 3 dc, ch 1) twice, skip
next dc, dc in last dc: 59 dc and
6 buttonholes (ch-1 sps).

**Row 4:** Ch 2, turn; dc in first dc
and in each dc and in each ch-1 sp
across: 65 dc.

**Row 5:** Ch 2, turn; dc in first dc and
in each dc across.

**Row 6:** Turn; slip st loosely in first 18 dc, ch 2, dc in next 29 dc, leave remaining 18 dc unworked: 29 dc.

**Rows 7-13** (Decrease rows): Ch 2, turn; beginning in first dc, dc2tog, dc in next dc and in each dc across to last 2 dc, dc2tog: 15 dc.

**Rows 14 and 15:** Ch 2, turn; dc in first dc and in each dc across.

**Rows 16-20** (Increase rows): Ch 2, turn; 2 dc in first dc, dc in next dc and in each dc across to last dc, 2 dc in last dc: 25 dc.

**Rows 21-28:** Ch 2, turn; dc in first dc and in each dc across; do **not** finish off.

# EDGING

**Rnd 1:** Ch 1, do **not** turn; sc evenly around entire piece *(Fig. 1, page 43)* working 3 sc in each corner; join with slip st to first sc, finish off.

**Rnd 2** (Right side): With **right** side facing, join Brown with sc in same st as joining *(Figs. 2a & b, page 44)*; sc in next sc and in each sc around working 3 sc in each corner sc; join with slip st to first sc, finish off.

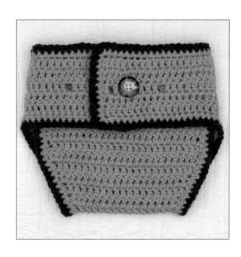

**BUTTONS & SNAPS PLACEMENT**

With **right** side facing, sew button to center of Row 26 (front). The front can be buttoned in any of the 3 buttonholes on each side for an adjustable fit.

Snaps are added to keep the corners of the last row in place. Sew a half snap on the **right** side of each corner of Row 28.

Button the diaper cover in the desired position, then sew the second half of each snap on the **wrong** side of Row 1 to correspond with the first half of the snap. For the diaper cover to be adjustable, the second half of 2 additional snaps may be sewn on each side of Row 1 to match the first half of the snap when the cover is buttoned in the remaining 2 buttonhole choices.

# Hat

With Gold, ch 4; join with slip st to form a ring.

**Rnd 1** (Right side)**:** Ch 2 (does **not** count as a dc, now and throughout), 12 dc in ring; join with slip st to first dc: 12 dc.

*Note:* Loop a short piece of yarn around any stitch to mark Rnd 1 as **right** side.

**Rnd 2:** Ch 2, do **not** turn; 2 dc in same st as joining and in each dc around; join with slip st to first dc: 24 dc.

**Rnd 3:** Ch 2, dc in same st as joining, 2 dc in next dc, (dc in next dc, 2 dc in next dc) around; join with slip st to first dc: 36 dc.

**Rnd 4:** Ch 2, dc in same st as joining and in next 2 dc, 2 dc in next dc, (dc in next 3 dc, 2 dc in next dc) around; join with slip st to first dc: 45 dc.

**Rnd 5:** Ch 2, dc in same st as joining and in each dc around; join with slip st to first dc.

Repeat Rnd 5, 6 times **or** until Hat measures desired length.

Finish off.

**Edging:** With **right** side facing, join Brown with sc in same st as joining *(Figs. 2a & b, page 44)*; sc in next dc and in each dc around; join with slip st to first sc, finish off.

## HORN (Make 2)

With Brown, ch 4; join with slip st to form a ring.

**Rnd 1** (Right side)**:** Ch 1, 8 sc in ring; join with slip st to first sc.

*Note:* Mark Rnd 1 as **right** side.

**Rnd 2:** Ch 1, do **not** turn; sc in same st as joining and in each sc around; cut Brown, insert hook in first sc, using Gold, YO and draw through st **and** through loop on hook.

**Rnds 3-7:** Ch 1, sc in same st as joining and in each sc around; join with slip st to first sc.

Finish off leaving a long end for sewing.

## EAR (Make 2)

With Gold, ch 4; join with slip st to form a ring.

**Rnd 1** (Right side)**:** Ch 2, 6 dc in ring; join with slip st to first dc.

*Note:* Mark Rnd 1 as **right** side.

**Rnd 2:** Ch 2, do **not** turn; dc in same st as joining, 2 dc in next dc, (dc in next dc, 2 dc in next dc) twice; join with slip st to first dc: 9 dc.

**Rnd 3:** Ch 2, dc in same st as joining and in next dc, 2 dc in next dc, (dc in next 2 dc, 2 dc in next dc) twice; join with slip st to first dc: 12 dc.

**Rnd 4:** Ch 2, dc in same st as joining and in next 2 dc, 2 dc in next dc, (dc in next 3 dc, 2 dc in next dc) twice; join with slip st to first dc: 15 dc.

**Rnd 5:** Ch 2, dc in same st as joining and in next 3 dc, 2 dc in next dc, (dc in next 4 dc, 2 dc in next dc) twice; join with slip st to first dc, finish off leaving a long end for sewing: 18 dc.

Lightly stuff Horns with fiberfill.

Using photo, page 39, as a guide for placement and long ends, sew Horns and Ears to Hat.

# GENERAL INSTRUCTIONS

## ABBREVIATIONS

| | |
|---|---|
| cm | centimeters |
| ch | chain(s) |
| dc | double crochet(s) |
| dc2tog | double crochet 2 together |
| hdc | half double crochet(s) |
| mm | millimeters |
| Rnd(s) | Round(s) |
| sc | single crochet(s) |
| sp(s) | space(s) |
| st(s) | stitch(es) |
| YO | yarn over |

| CROCHET TERMINOLOGY | | |
|---|---|---|
| UNITED STATES | | INTERNATIONAL |
| slip stitch (slip st) | = | single crochet (sc) |
| single crochet (sc) | = | double crochet (dc) |
| half double crochet (hdc) | = | half treble crochet (htr) |
| double crochet (dc) | = | treble crochet(tr) |
| treble crochet (tr) | = | double treble crochet (dtr) |
| double treble crochet (dtr) | = | triple treble crochet (ttr) |
| triple treble crochet (tr tr) | = | quadruple treble crochet (qtr) |
| skip | = | miss |

## SYMBOLS & TERMS

★ — work instructions following ★ as many **more** times as indicated in addition to the first time.

( ) or [ ]— work enclosed instructions **as many** times as specified by the number immediately following **or** contains explanatory remarks.

colon (:) — the number(s) given after a colon at the end of a row or round denote(s) the number of stitches or spaces you should have on that row or round.

| CROCHET HOOKS | | | | | | | | | | | | | | | |
|---|---|---|---|---|---|---|---|---|---|---|---|---|---|---|---|
| U.S. | B-1 | C-2 | D-3 | E-4 | F-5 | G-6 | H-8 | I-9 | J-10 | K-10½ | L-11 | M/N-13 | N/P-15 | P/Q | Q | S |
| Metric - mm | 2.25 | 2.75 | 3.25 | 3.5 | 3.75 | 4 | 5 | 5.5 | 6 | 6.5 | 8 | 9 | 10 | 15 | 16 | 19 |

| Yarn Weight Symbol & Names | LACE ( 0 ) | SUPER FINE ( 1 ) | FINE ( 2 ) | LIGHT ( 3 ) | MEDIUM ( 4 ) | BULKY ( 5 ) | SUPER BULKY ( 6 ) |
|---|---|---|---|---|---|---|---|
| Type of Yarns in Category | Fingering, 10-count crochet thread | Sock, Fingering Baby | Sport, Baby | DK, Light Worsted | Worsted, Afghan, Aran | Chunky, Craft, Rug | Bulky, Roving |
| Crochet Gauge* Ranges in Single Crochet to 4" (10 cm) | 32-42 double crochets** | 21-32 sts | 16-20 sts | 12-17 sts | 11-14 sts | 8-11 sts | 5-9 sts |
| Advised Hook Size Range | Steel*** 6,7,8 Regular hook B-1 | B-1 to E-4 | E-4 to 7 | 7 to I-9 | I-9 to K-10.5 | K-10.5 to M-13 | M-13 and larger |

*GUIDELINES ONLY: The chart above reflects the most commonly used gauges and hook sizes for specific yarn categories.

** Lace weight yarns are usually crocheted on larger-size hooks to create lacy openwork patterns. Accordingly, a gauge range is difficult to determine. Always follow the gauge stated in your pattern.

*** Steel crochet hooks are sized differently from regular hooks–the higher the number the smaller the hook, which is the reverse of regular hook sizing.

| | |
|---|---|
| ■□□□ **BEGINNER** | Projects for first-time crocheters using basic stitches. Minimal shaping. |
| ■■□□ **EASY** | Projects using yarn with basic stitches, repetitive stitch patterns, simple color changes, and simple shaping and finishing. |
| ■■■□ **INTERMEDIATE** | Projects using a variety of techniques, such as basic lace patterns or color patterns, mid-level shaping and finishing. |
| ■■■■ **EXPERIENCED** | Projects with intricate stitch patterns, techniques and dimension, such as non-repeating patterns, multi-color techniques, fine threads, small hooks, detailed shaping and refined finishing. |

## GAUGE

Exact gauge is essential for proper fit. Before beginning your project, make the sample swatch given in the individual instructions in the yarn and hook specified. After completing the swatch, measure it, counting your stitches and rows carefully. If your swatch is larger or smaller than specified, **make another, changing hook size to get the correct gauge**. Keep trying until you find the size hook that will give you the specified gauge.

## FREE LOOPS OF A CHAIN

When instructed to work in free loops of a chain, work in loop indicated by arrow *(Fig. 1)*.

**Fig. 1**

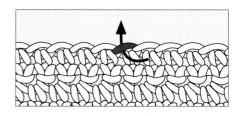

## JOINING WITH SC

When instructed to join with sc, begin with a slip knot on hook. Insert hook in stitch indicated, YO and pull up a loop, YO and draw through both loops on hook *(Figs. 2a & b)*.

**Fig. 2a**

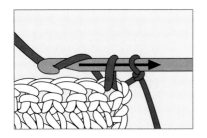

**Fig. 2b**

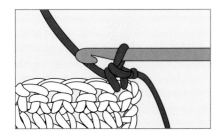

## JOINING WITH DC

When instructed to join with dc, begin with a slip knot on hook. YO, holding loop on hook, insert hook in stitch indicated, YO and pull up a loop (3 loops on hook), (YO and draw through 2 loops on hook) twice *(Fig. 3)*.

**Fig. 3**

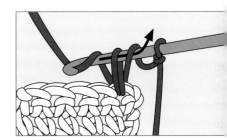

# TASSEL

Cut a piece of cardboard 3" (7.5 cm) square.
Wind a double strand of yarn around the cardboard approximately 10 times. Cut an 18" (45.5 cm) length of yarn and insert it under all of the strands at the top of the cardboard; pull up tightly and tie securely. Leave the yarn ends long enough to attach the tassel. Cut the yarn at the opposite end of the cardboard (*Fig. 4a*) and then remove the cardboard.
Cut a 6" (15 cm) length of yarn and wrap it tightly around the tassel twice, 1" (2.5 cm) below the top (*Fig. 4b*); tie securely. Trim the ends.

Fig. 4a

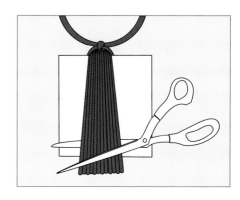

Fig. 4b

# EMBROIDERY STITCHES
## SATIN STITCH

Satin stitch is a series of straight stitches worked side-by-side so they touch but do not overlap *(Fig. 5a)* **or** by coming out of and going into the same stitch *(Fig. 5b)*. Come up at odd numbers and go down at even numbers.

**Fig. 5a**

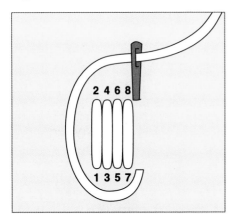

**Fig. 5b**

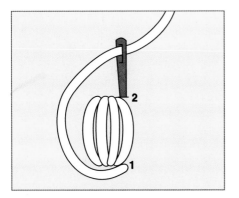

## STRAIGHT STITCH

Straight stitch is just what the name implies, a single, straight stitch. Come up at 1 and go down at 2 *(Fig. 6)*.

**Fig. 6**

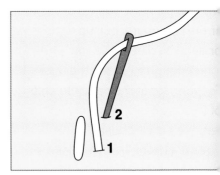

# YARN INFORMATION

Each item in this book was made using Medium Weight Yarn. Any brand of Medium Weight Yarn may be used. It is best to refer to the yardage/meters when determining how many balls or skeins to purchase. Remember, to arrive at the finished size, it is the GAUGE/TENSION that is important, not the brand of yarn.

For your convenience, listed below are the specific yarns used to create our photography models.

### BUNNY SET
*Caron® Simply Soft®*
White - #9701 White
Pink - #9719 Soft Pink
Black - #9727 Black

### CHICK SET
*Red Heart® Super Saver®*
Yellow - #0324 Bright Yellow
Orange - #0254 Pumpkin

### PUPPY SET
*Red Heart® Super Saver®*
Ecru - #4313 Aran Fleck
Brown - #0366 Warm Brown
Black - #0312 Black

### LADYBUG SET
*Red Heart® Super Saver®*
Red - #0319 Cherry Red
Black - #0312 Black

### GIRAFFE SET
*Red Heart® Super Saver®*
Gold - #0321 Gold
Brown - #0336 Warm Brown

PLEASE SHARE
your comments and suggestions at
www.facebook.com/Official.LeisureArts

PLUS you can find us on Twitter,
Pinterest and YouTube too!!

Production Team: Writer/Technical Editor - Cathy Hardy; Editorial Writer - Susan Frantz Wiles; Senior Graphic Artist - Lora Puls; Graphic Artist - Jessica Bramlett; Photo Stylist - Sondra Danie and Photographer - Ken West.

We have made every effort to ensure that these instructions are accurate and complete. We cannot, however, be responsible for human error, typographical mistakes, or variations in individual work.